JELLYFISH

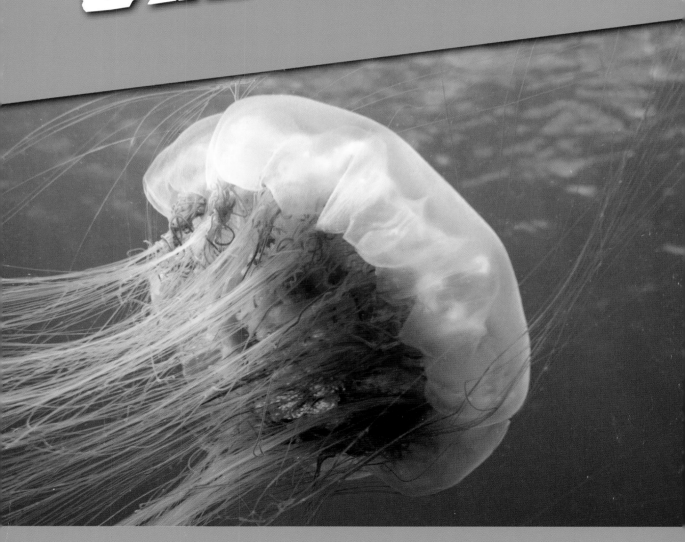

▲ SUSAN H. GRAY

CHERRY
LAKE
Publishing

Published in the United States of America by Cherry Lake Publishing
Ann Arbor, Michigan
www.cherrylakepublishing.com

Consultants: Dominique A. Didier, PhD, Associate Professor, Department of Biology, Millersville University;
Marla Conn, ReadAbility, Inc.
Book design: Sleeping Bear Press

Photo Credits: ©Steven Melanson/Dreamstime.com, cover, 1, 9; ©Cigdem Sean Cooper/Dreamstime.com, 5; ©Rich
Carey/Shutterstock Images, 6; ©Dorling Kindersley RF/Thinkstock, 11, 25; ©Matt Antonino/Dreamstime.com, 13;
©Daleen Loest/Shutterstock Images, 14; ©iStockphoto/Thinkstock, 15, 20, 21; ©lsantilli/Shutterstock Images, 17;
©Arabesk/iStockphoto, 19; ©Hidden Ocean 2005 Expedition: NOAA Office of Ocean Exploration/http://www.flickr.
com/CC-BY-2.0, 23; ©Tammy616/iStockphoto, 27; ©Vilainecrevette/Shutterstock Images, 29

Library of Congress Cataloging-in-Publication Data

Gray, Susan Heinrichs.
Jellyfish / by Susan H. Gray.
      pages cm. — (Exploring our oceans)
   Summary: "Includes facts about jellyfish, including physical features, habitat, life cycle, food, and threats to these ocean
creatures. Photos, captions, and keywords supplement the narrative of this informational text"— Provided by publisher.
   Audience: 8-12.
   Audience: Grade 4 to 6.
   Includes bibliographical references and index.
   ISBN 978-1-62431-600-5 (hardcover) — ISBN 978-1-62431-612-8 (pbk.)
   — ISBN 978-1-62431-624-1 (pdf) — ISBN 978-1-62431-636-4 (ebook)
   1. Jellyfishes—Juvenile literature. I. Title.

   QL377.S4G727 2014
   593.5'3—dc23   2013031301

Cherry Lake Publishing would like to acknowledge the work of
The Partnership for 21st Century Skills. Please visit *www.p21.org*
for more information.

Printed in the United States of America
Corporate Graphics Inc.
January 2014

ABOUT THE AUTHOR

Susan H. Gray has a master's degree in zoology. She has worked in research and has taught
college-level science classes. Susan has also written more than 140 science and reference books,
but especially likes to write about animals. She and her husband, Michael, live in Cabot, Arkansas.

TABLE OF CONTENTS

A SEA OF JELLY

It was summertime, and the jellyfish were drifting north. Thousands of them floated in the waters around Japan. They were enormous—bigger and heavier than washing machines. They bumped and pushed one another as they drifted. Their bodies pulsed as they moved along. Their stinging **tentacles** dangled beneath them. As they plowed into one another, their stinging cells sometimes fired. Normally, a jellyfish sting might **paralyze** or kill another animal. But not a single jelly was harmed.

[21ST CENTURY SKILLS LIBRARY]

This cauliflower jellyfish is sometimes eaten as a delicacy in Japan and China or used to make medicine.

Too many jellyfish in the water near beaches can be dangerous for swimmers.

Jellyfish swarms like this are becoming more common in Japan. But jellies have always lived in the waters nearby. Japan is not the only place where jellies show up. They appear in every ocean on earth. Most swim in the open water, but some rest quietly in the shallows, and some even rest on the bottom. Certain **species** prefer cold temperatures. They spend their lives in Arctic or Antarctic seas. Others prefer the scalding water of deep-sea volcanic vents.

Jellyfish are among the great success stories of the animal world. Scientists have found **fossils** of jellylike animals. The fossils were in rocks that were more than 500 million years old. Jellyfish might have been here millions of years before the dinosaurs!

THINK ABOUT IT

JELLYFISH SWARMS OCCUR IN MANY DIFFERENT PLACES AROUND THE WORLD. BUT PEOPLE ARE USUALLY NOT PLEASED TO SEE THEM. WHY MIGHT THAT BE?

THE JELLYFISH BODY

Scientists tell us that many different kinds of jellylike animals exist. But the "true jellyfish" have round bodies and live in the ocean. The body of a true jellyfish is a dome, called the bell. Several structures hang beneath it. All of the animal's organs are arranged in a circular pattern. Scientists call this **radial symmetry**. This arrangement allows the jelly to move and respond in any direction.

Jellyfish come in many shapes and sizes. The moon jelly for instance, has a flattened bell, while the cannonball jelly has a globe shape. One of the smallest jellies is the sea thimble, with its little thumb-size bell. The giant bell of the lion's mane jellyfish can grow more than 7 feet (2.1 m) across. This jelly would cover a king-size bed!

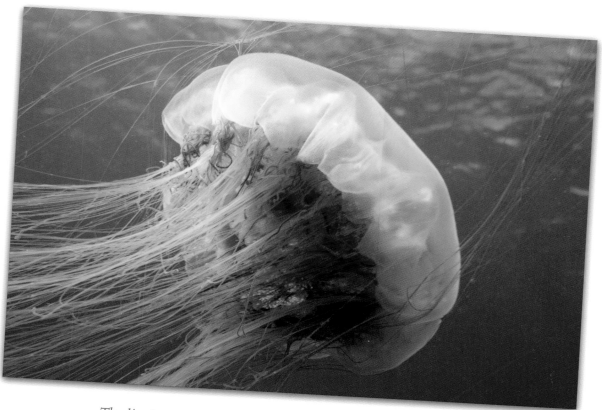

The lion's mane jellyfish is just one of about 200 jellyfish species.

Some jellies have faintly colored bodies. Others, such as the compass jellyfish and the purple-striped jelly, have colored markings. But most jellies are not colorful animals. They are usually whitish or transparent. This makes them almost invisible in the water.

The bell has an outer tissue layer, an inner tissue layer, and a soft jellylike material in between. The soft material is called the mesoglea. Within the mesoglea are muscles, nerves, and reproductive organs. There is also a cavity for digestion.

Muscles lie only within the rim of the bell. When these muscles contract, the rim draws inward. When they relax, the rim spreads out. This action creates the animal's swimming motion.

A nerve net is spread throughout the mesoglea. Sensors on the body send signals to the nerves, and the nerves cause the muscles to contract. Some sensors detect light and chemicals. Others relay messages about the jelly's position. They help the animal to stay upright.

BODY DIAGRAM

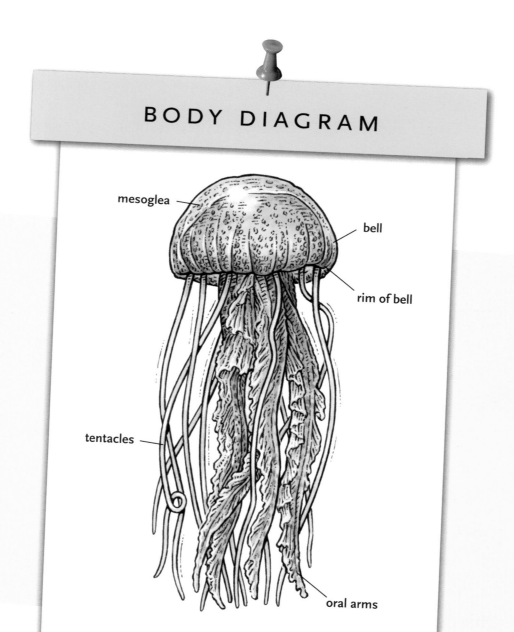

mesoglea

bell

rim of bell

tentacles

oral arms

Most jellyfish live less than one year.

Like the jelly's other organs, the reproductive organs are arranged in a circle. They are sometimes the most visible part of the jellyfish body. These organs produce **sperm** or egg cells.

The mouth is on the underside of the bell. It is surrounded by thick, dangling oral arms. They help transport food to the mouth. After food enters the body, it moves into the digestive cavity. There, it is broken down. Food is carried to the rest of the mesoglea through a system of canals. Sweeping the food along are thousands of tiny, hairlike **cilia**. Food that is not digested goes back out through the mouth.

Tentacles hang beneath the bell. They may be very short or quite long. In the moon jellyfish, tentacles form a little fringe around the rim. In the lion's mane jellyfish, they reach lengths of 100 feet (30.5 m) or more. The tentacles are loaded with stinging cells. They are used for defense and also for catching prey.

Jellyfish vary both in size and in color.

LOOK AGAIN

LOOK CLOSELY AT THIS PHOTOGRAPH. JELLYFISH CANNOT "OUTRUN" THEIR ENEMIES. SO HOW MIGHT THEY DEAL WITH DANGER?

There are about 200 known species of true jellyfish. But there are many other species of jellylike creatures. The box jellies, for instance, are not true jellies. They are shaped like cubes and are stronger swimmers than the true jellies. Some box jellies have only four tentacles, while others have four clusters of tentacles. These animals are among the deadliest creatures on earth.

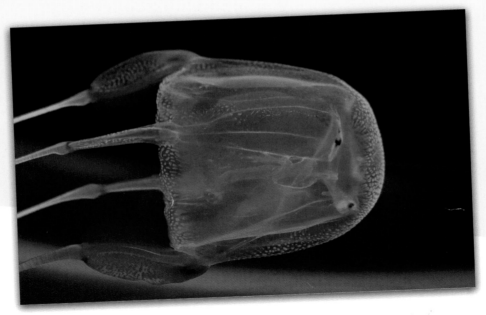

Each tentacle on a box jelly has about 5,000 stinging cells.

The Portuguese man-of-war floats on the surface of warm ocean waters.

The Portuguese man-of-war is another jellylike animal. Although it looks like a jellyfish, it is actually a group of individuals of the same species. In these creatures, one individual may form the float, an air-filled sac the animal deflates and inflates in order to sink or rise in the water. Other individuals may serve as tentacles or other organs.

The tiny freshwater jellies are also not true jellyfish. They live in lakes and rivers around the world. These dime-size animals have life cycles that are very different from the true jellies.

CHAPTER 3

How Jellies Fill Their Bellies

Jellyfish are predators, eating other sea animals. They devour small fish, shrimp, **plankton**, and other jellies. Their tentacles and oral arms may entrap their victims. But their stinging cells are the real weapons.

Each stinging cell contains a little capsule called the nematocyst. The nematocyst is covered by a **microscopic** trapdoor. Just inside the trapdoor is a long coiled tube covered with venomous, or poisonous, spines. The tube is actually turned inside out so the spines are on the inside. When a prey animal brushes by, the nematocysts spring into action. The trapdoors fling open, and the spiny tubes shoot out. As they do this, they turn right side out so the spines are exposed. The tubes shoot into the victim and release their venom.

Jellyfish are carnivores. They eat other animals.

Jellies do not eat members of their own species. When they bump into one another, their nematocysts fail to fire. Even if they did, it would not harm the other jellies. They are like other venomous animals in this respect. These animals are not harmed by the venom of their own species.

It is different with prey animals, though. The venom is enough to paralyze or kill them. The venom has to be strong and act quickly. Many jellyfish are delicate animals. Struggling fish could easily tear up their bodies.

Once the jelly's prey is unable to move, the jelly's oral arms move the prey toward the mouth. From the mouth, the prey moves into the digestive cavity. There, it is broken down and moved along the canals.

Some jellyfish have very different feeding methods. Cassiopea is a jelly that rests upside down in shallow water. Its frilly oral arms wave back and forth in the sunlight. Cassiopea has algae living in its body. In the light, the algae produce food to nourish their own cells and to feed the jellyfish.

The Australian spotted jellyfish's poison is weak.
These jellies do not pose a threat to swimmers.

These moon jellyfish are prey for birds, sea turtles, some fish, and other jellyfish.

The lagoon jellyfish has no tentacles but has many mouths along its oral arms. It draws food into the mouths that then moves into digestive canals inside the arms. The moon jellies have sticky oral arms. They trap tiny plankton animals and move them toward the digestive canals.

Actually, jellyfish themselves are plankton. Most are weak swimmers, which is common in plankton. Jellies have only weak control of their horizontal movements. They go wherever the waves or currents push them.

However, they can control their vertical position, like many other plankton animals. Jellies sink to great depths in the daytime. There, in the dark waters, they are less likely to be seen and eaten. At night, though, it is a different story. These animals rise toward the surface to feed.

A jellyfish's mouth is a small opening located on the underside of the bell. Jellyfish waste comes out this same opening.

LOOK AGAIN

THIS JELLYFISH HAS NO BRIGHT MARKINGS. HOW MIGHT THAT HELP IT TO CATCH PREY?

CHAPTER 4

JELLYFISH LIFE CYCLE

Most people are familiar with the swimming, umbrella-shaped jellyfish. It is called a medusa. The medusa's life cycle, like that of all jellyfish, involves several stages.

The female medusae produce egg cells, and males produce sperm cells. At some point, the males release their cells into the water. The females may either release their egg cells or retain them in their bodies. Either way, the sperm cells eventually unite with them.

Two united cells develop into a simple animal called a **planula** larva. It is a tiny, swimming creature covered in cilia. Slowly, it makes its way to the seafloor. There, it glues itself to a solid object such as a rock or a clamshell.

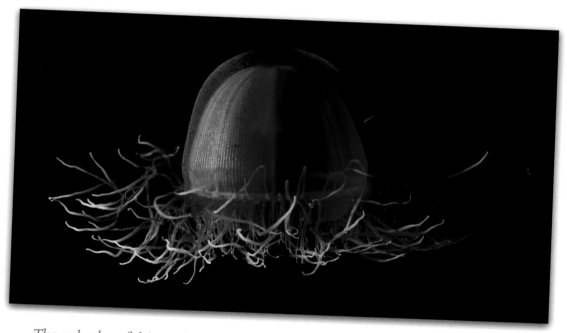

The red color of this medusa jellyfish would not be visible in deep ocean waters.

The larva grows and soon lengthens into a **polyp**. The polyp remains attached to the seafloor. It has a mouth surrounded by a circle of tentacles. The tentacles snag bits of food that drift by and drag them toward the mouth.

As the polyp continues to grow, it comes to look like a stack of dishes. In time, the "dishes," known as ephyrae, peel from the stack and float away. Each one is tiny and round and has the basic body plan of the medusa. Soon, it develops the bell, nerve net, oral arms, and other structures.

GO DEEPER

PLANULA LARVAE PREFER TO LATCH ON TO HARD SURFACES. CAN YOU THINK OF ANY ADVANTAGE THIS MIGHT BE?

LIFE CYCLE

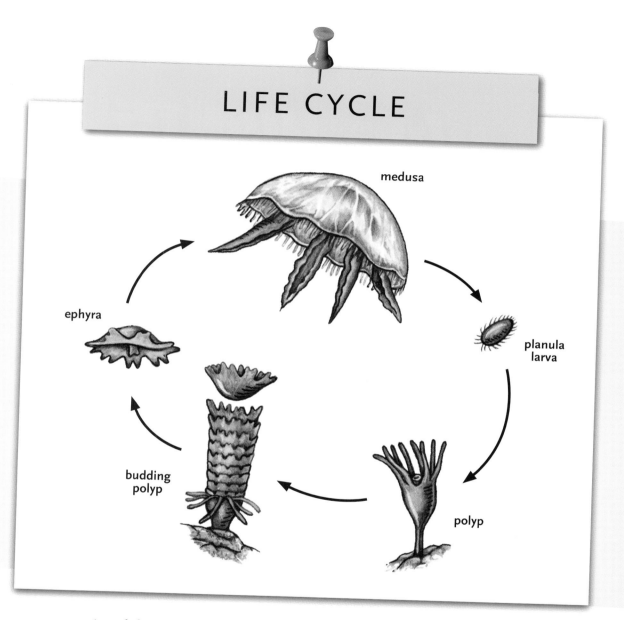

An adult jellyfish is a medusa named after the mythological creature, Medusa, who had snakes on her head instead of hair.

WHO WANTS A JELLY?

Not many predators go after jellyfish. This is because jellies are not the easiest animals to deal with. First, the predators have to find them. Many jellies are almost invisible in water. Plus they drift downward in the daytime, becoming even harder to spot. A predator must also deal with the stinging nematocysts. Finally, predators will waste energy catching and eating jellyfish. The jellies are composed almost entirely of water. So predators won't get much nutrition from such prey.

[21ST CENTURY SKILLS LIBRARY]

Unfortunately, many sea turtles mistake floating plastic bags for jellyfish. Turtles are harmed and sometimes die after eating the plastic.

Still, the jellies have their enemies. Sea turtles, birds, fish, and other jellyfish species feed on them. These animals seem to be immune to the jelly's sting.

Jellyfish sometimes face other dangers. They often get stuck in fishing nets. They also are sucked into pipes at seaside power plants.

Jellyfish populations, though, are not threatened. No species of true jellyfish is in danger of dying out. In fact, in some places, there are too many jellyfish.

Thousands of jellyfish sometimes group together and form swarms. Swarms occur when many jellies mature at the same time. This is not unusual. After all, a jellyfish can produce thousands of egg or sperm cells at once. This results in thousands of larvae and thousands of medusae.

Jellyfish swarms seem to be occurring more often. Near Japan, swarms used to be a rare sight. Now, Japanese scientists report swarms almost every year.

Perhaps overfishing is causing more swarms. Many fish compete with jellies for available food. If those fish are removed, the jellies will have more to eat and their population will swell.

Other factors might be involved. Right now, experts are looking at many possible causes. Some think rising water temperatures might be to blame. Others are investigating levels of ocean pollution. Still others worry that jellies are moving into new environments. There is much to learn about these animals. Scientists have plenty of work to do. ◢

Purple-striped jellyfish like this one can often be seen in public aquariums.

LOOK AGAIN

WHAT DOES THIS PHOTOGRAPH REVEAL ABOUT THIS JELLYFISH'S **HABITAT**?

THINK ABOUT IT

- Jellyfish swarms can sometimes cause problems for fishing fleets and power plants. What other businesses might be hurt by swarms?

- Chapter 2 points out that true jellyfish have radial symmetry. The Portuguese man-of-war does not have radial symmetry. Why would people think it is a jellyfish?

- What did you learn about jellyfish that surprised you?

- In chapter 3, we learned that nematocysts react with lightning speed. Why do nematocysts have to fire so quickly?

- Chapter 4 covers the jellyfish life cycle. Can you explain how one larva might produce 10 or 20 medusae?

LEARN MORE

FURTHER READING

Gowell, Elizabeth. *Amazing Jellies: Jewels of the Sea.* Piermont, NH: Bunker Hill Publishing, 2007.

Gray, Susan H. *Australian Spotted Jellyfish.* Ann Arbor, MI: Cherry Lake Publishing, 2010.

Sexton, Colleen. *The Box Jellyfish.* Minneapolis: Bellwether Media, 2011.

WEB SITES

Discovery Kids—Are Jellyfish Really Fish?
http://kids.discovery.com/tell-me/animals/fish/are-jellyfish-really-fish
This Web page has basic information about jellies, their swimming habits, and stinging cells.

Monterey Bay Aquarium—Jellywatch
www.jellywatch.org/blooms/facts
Learn about the people studying jellyfish swarms, as well as basic information about jellies and a number of fun facts.

National Geographic Kids—Jellyfish
http://kids.nationalgeographic.com/kids/animals/creaturefeature/jellyfish
Learn more information and fun facts about jellyfish, and watch a video about these sea creatures.

GLOSSARY

cilia (SILL-ee-uh) tiny hairlike structures that wave rhythmically to sweep objects forward

fossils (FOS-uhlz) remains of long-dead plants or animals

habitat (HAB-i-tat) the place where an animal or plant naturally lives

microscopic (mye-kruh-SKAH-pik) so small it can only be seen with a microscope

paralyze (PA-ruh-lize) to stop all movement or feeling

plankton (PLANGK-tuhn) aquatic plant and animal life that drifts or that has only weak swimming motions

planula (PLAN-yuh-luh) the cilia-covered swimming young of a jellyfish

polyp (POL-ip) a very small animal with an attached base, a stalk, and tentacles

radial symmetry (REY-dee-uhl SIM-i-tree) a basic body plan in which structures and organs are arranged in a circle

species (SPEE-sheez) one type, or kind, of plant or animal

sperm (SPURM) male reproductive cell

tentacles (TEN-tuh-kuhlz) slender, flexible limbs or appendages in an animal, used for grasping or moving around, or containing sense organs

INDEX